TEST YOUR CHILD'S

English Grammar

Boswell Taylor

eadway · Hodder & Stoughton

Notes for Parents and Teachers

This is a work book. Each double page is concerned with one of the parts of speech that are the elements of the English language. The rule is given, explained with examples, and exercises follow. Special tests are provided which are prefaced with ★ Now test yourself. Answers to these tests are given at the end of the book. The final test has a rating chart so that the student can estimate his or her degree of success.

Grammar in the widest sense of the word is both the science and the art of language. There is no such thing as 'standard English'. There is an accepted standard, but even this is not fixed. It allows for variations, and it is for ever changing because the English language is a living language and new uses of words are constantly being accepted. This book is concerned with the main structure of the English language which is based on the parts of speech. The work may well confirm grammar rules that are observed already. It should help to correct faults that may not have been realised previously, but perhaps its major result will be to give greater confidence in the daily use of the vital means of communication. To make best use of this book a dictionary is needed. The *Oxford Paperback Dictionary* can be recommended, or the *Concise Oxford Dictionary*, although the majority of dictionaries will provide the help that is needed.

Contents

Facts about the parts of speech

We speak and write the English language. The structure that provides the word patterns is known as grammar. When we study grammar, we study how words are put together to form sentences. We rarely think about sentences or grammar when we speak and write. The words fall naturally into some sort of pattern. Sometimes the pattern is correct, and sometimes it is not. The use of correct grammar means that the correct meaning is conveyed. Incorrect grammar introduces confusion to the word patterns.

Word patterns are composed of parts of speech. Each part of speech has its own special function. There are eight (some say nine)* separate functions or jobs; there are eight parts of speech. Here they are:

Part of speech	Function	Examples
Noun	naming word	sausage, Jack
Pronoun	substitute for noun	she, he, it, they
Verb	doing word	walk, think
Adjective	describing word	proud, beautiful
Adverb	word modifying action	run *quickly*, work *late*
Preposition	relates one thing to another	ship *on* the sea, jump *over* the wall
Conjunction	joining word	the driver *and* the conductor
Interjection	expresses emotion	Oh! Oh!

* Sometimes the three 'articles' *a*, *an* (indefinite) and *the* (definite) are called a part of speech.

Every word in this book and in every book belongs to one of the parts of speech.

Nouns

A noun is the name of a person, animal, place or thing. Everything has a name, such as chair, ship, football. Everybody has a name. There is the common name, such as person. Boy and girl are nouns to tell us the kind of person. Then every boy and every girl has a proper name, such as William or Emma. All the words printed in colour are nouns.

Underline each noun in the following sentences:

A 1 I patted a <u>dog</u>, stroked a <u>cat</u>, rode on an <u>elephant</u>, and fed a <u>seal</u>.

   2 I sat on a chair, drank from a cup, ate off a plate, and used a spoon.

   3 I played in the park, sailed a ship, built a sand-castle, and flew a kite.

   4 I played football with William, John, Fred, and Craig.

Write the most suitable noun from the list in each empty space:
snake, horse, lion, mouse, sparrow, frog

B 1 The... *mouse* .... squeaked.   2 The .... neighed.

   3 The .... hissed.   4 The .... croaked.

   5 The .... chirped.   6 The .... roared.

Singular and Plural (Number)

Nouns can have either singular ('one') or plural ('more than one') number. Generally the plural is formed by adding -s or -es to the singular, but there are exceptions. In the exercise below, all the words are exceptions to the rule. Some words, like sheep, are both singular and plural.

Fill the gaps to complete the chart.

	Singular	Plural		Singular	Plural
C 1	knife	*Knives*	2	....	thieves
3	child	....	4	....	geese
5	tooth	....	6	....	sheep

Nouns – Gender

Gender concerns the two sexes, male and female.
Masculine gender denotes the male sex, as man, father, boy.
Feminine gender denotes the female sex, such as woman, mother, girl.
We also have Neuter gender and Common gender.
Neuter gender denotes things without sex, such as ball, church.
Common gender denotes either sex, such as child, person, teacher.

Fill the gaps to complete the chart:

		Masculine	Feminine			Masculine	Feminine
A	1	*abbot*	abbess		2	god	. . . .
	3	master	. . . .		4	. . . .	nun
	5	. . . .	spinster		6	gander	. . . .
	7	emperor	. . . .		8	. . . .	lady
	9	. . . .	princess		10	husband	. . . .
	11	nephew	. . . .		12	. . . .	witch
	13	. . . .	ewe		14	stallion	. . . .
	15	buck	. . . .		16	. . . .	bitch
	17	. . . .	landlady		18	uncle	. . . .
	19	son-in-law	. . . .		20	. . . .	hind

Change all masculines to corresponding feminines in the following:

B 1   The wizard changed the prince to a frog.

   The witch changed the princess to a frog. . . . .

   2   The king awarded a medal to the hero.

   . . . .

   3   The page followed the bridegroom into the church.

   . . . .

   4   On to the stage leapt the actor to stab the villain.

   . . . .

   5   The heir to the whole estate was a bachelor.

   . . . .

Gender

Common gender words are uni-sex words. The same word is both male and female.
Neuter gender denotes things that have neither sex nor even life.
Here are 49 nouns. *Underline* the 25 words with Common gender.
Cross out the 24 words with Neuter gender.

A <u>child</u>   ~~chair~~   <u>friend</u>   <u>parent</u>   ~~school~~   <u>scholar</u>   <u>pig</u>

house	mountain	deer	volcano	singer	owner	window
passenger	pop-song	explorer	swimmer	ladder	radio-set	sheep
fowl	boots	librarian	desk	book	bird	ice-cream
people	road	animal	sausage	onlookers	balloon	choir
rain	dagger	journalist	mob	thunder	reader	coal
car	canal	sovereign	canoe	fish	door	lemonade

Families

A sheep can be a ewe (female), a ram (male) or a lamb (young animal).
These are the names (nouns) of the members of nine families all jumbled up:
lion, bitch, foal, bull, mare, piglet, sow, stallion, duckling, drake, cock, goose,
cub, cow, buck, lioness, gosling, puppy, dog, gander, boar, calf, duck, chicken,
fawn, hen, doe

Use names from the list above to complete the chart to make happy families.

	Male	Female	Young animal
B 1	lion	lioness	cub
2	gander		
3			piglet
4		bitch	
5	drake		
6		mare	
7			fawn
8	bull		
9		hen	

Group Terms or Collective Nouns

A collective noun names a group of individuals as if they were one individual:

committee (of people)   herd (of cattle)   pack (of cards)

They may be singular or plural:

one team of players   two teams of players
The committee is made up of boys and girls.
The committee are quarrelling among themselves again.

Special group terms are used with both animate (living) and inanimate (non-living) things.
These are collective nouns:

crew, choir, flock, gang, company, swarm, litter, stud, shoal, school

Fill the gaps with the correct collective noun.

Animate (*living things*)

A 1 ...*litter*.......of puppies   2 .... of sailors

   3 .... of birds   4 .... of actors

   5 .... of thieves   6 .... of whales

   7 .... of herring   8 .... of singers

   9 .... of horses   10 .... of bees

These are collective nouns:

library, suit, crate, fleet, bunch, bouquet, string, chest, bundle, set

Fill the gaps with the correct collective noun.

Inanimate (*things without animal life*)

B 1 .*bouquet*..... of flowers   2 .... of books

   3 .... of beads   4 .... of clothes

   5 .... of grapes   6 .... of drawers

   7 .... of tools   8 .... of ships

   9 .... of rags   10 .... of fruit

★ Now test yourself in the use of nouns

Write the singular of the following:

A 1 children . . . .   2 geese . . . .   3 boxes . . . .

   4 men . . . .   5 passers-by . . . .   6 teeth . . . .

Write the plural of the following:

B 1 woman . . . .   2 sheep . . . .   3 loaf . . . .

   4 echo . . . .   5 mouse-trap . . . .   6 foot . . . .

Write the masculine equivalent of the following:

C 1 goddess . . . .   2 wife . . . .   3 bride . . . .

   4 empress . . . .   5 niece . . . .   6 female . . . .

Write the feminine equivalent of the following:

D 1 lion . . . .   2 uncle . . . .   3 wizard . . . .

   4 traitor . . . .   5 monk . . . .   6 headmaster . . . .

Complete the chart to make happy families:

Male	Female	Young	Male	Female	Young
E 1 leopard	. . . .	. . . .	2	sow	. . . .
3 ram	. . . .	. . . .	4	. . . .	calf

Fill the gaps with the correct collective nouns:

F 1 . . . . of soldiers   2 . . . . of cattle

   3 . . . . of sheep   4 . . . . of wolves

   5 . . . . of eggs   6 . . . . of aeroplanes

   7 . . . . of hay   8 . . . . of furniture

Write the most appropriate word for a number of people:

G 1 at a music concert . . . .   2 in church . . . .

   3 in a bus . . . .   4 in a supermarket . . . .

Write one word for a number of things:

H 1 . . . . of bananas   2 . . . . of bells

   3 . . . . of strawberries   4 . . . . of islands

Pronouns

Pronouns are used in place of nouns. Look at these sentences:

Peter caught the ball. Peter bounced the ball Peter kicked the ball upfield.

There is too much repetition. We can use 'he' instead of 'Peter' and 'it' instead of 'ball', like this:

Peter caught the ball. He bounced it. He kicked it upfield.

We cannot change the name 'Peter' to 'he' in the first sentence, or 'ball' to 'it' or we would not know to whom 'he' referred and to what 'it' referred. A pronoun must always have a noun nearby to which it refers.

There are seven personal pronouns. They are the 'doers':

I   you   he   she   it   we   they

Each one makes sense if it is used to complete this sentence: . . . . . saw Jean.

I saw Jean.	You saw Jean.	He saw Jean.	She saw Jean.
It saw Jean.	We saw Jean.	They saw Jean.	

Each of these 'doers' has a 'receiver'. Something happens to it.

me   you   him   her   it   us   them

Each one makes sense if it is used to complete this sentence: Jean saw . . . . .

In each of the following you are given the 'doer' (the subjective). Put the correct 'receiver' (the objective) in the gap.

A 1 I saw Jean. Jean saw .. *me* . . . . .   2 You saw Jean. Jean saw . . . . . .

  3 He saw Jean. Jean saw . . . .   4 She saw Jean. Jean saw . . . . . .

  5 It saw Jean. Jean saw . . . .   6 We saw Jean. Jean saw . . . . . .

  7 They saw Jean. Jean saw . . . .

Write these sentences. Use pronouns instead of the nouns shown in *italics*.

B 1 Duncan went to the circus. *Duncan* went with his friends.

  Duncan went to the circus. He went with his friends.

  2 Delia plays tennis. *Delia* is good at the game.

  . . . .

  3 The snake saw the bird. *The snake* glided away.

  . . . .

Each of the personal pronouns has a possessive pronoun. These are the 'owners':

Nominative ('doers'):   I   you   he   she   it   we   you   they
Objective ('receivers'):   me   you   him   her   it   us   you   them
Possessive ('owners'):   mine   yours   his   hers   its   ours   yours   theirs

Complete the following, adding the correct possessive pronouns:

A 1 I bought the bike. It is my bike. The bike is . . . . . .

   2 You bought the bike. It is your bike. The bike is . . . . . .

   3 He bought the bike. It is his bike. The bike is . . . . . .

   4 She bought the bike. It is her bike. The bike is . . . . . .

   5 The dog caught the ball. It is its ball. The ball is . . . . . .

   6 We bought the books. They are our books. The books are . . . . . .

   7 They bought the books. They are their books. The books are . . . . . .

We can add 'self' or 'selves' to a personal pronoun to make a compound pronoun. Such compound pronouns are called reflexive pronouns because they look back on themselves.

myself   yourself   himself   herself   itself   ourselves   themselves

Complete the following, adding the correct reflexive pronoun:

B 1 I feed . .myself. . . .   2 You feed . . . .   3 He feeds . . . .

   4 She feeds . . . .   5 It feeds . . . .   6 We feed . . . .

   7 They feed . . . .

Three pronouns are used to ask questions. They are called interrogative (questioning) pronouns. They are: Who? Which? What?

Complete the following, adding the correct interrogative pronouns:

C 1 Who. . are you? I am Moira.

   2 . . . . class are you in? I am in Class Two.

   3 . . . . is your name? My name is Moira O'Farrell.

These pronouns (called definite pronouns) answer the question 'Which?':

this   these   that   those

Complete the following, adding the correct definite pronouns:

D 1 Which cake is yours? This is my cake, ... cake is his.

   2 Which buns are yours? . . . . . . are our buns, ... buns are theirs.

10

★ Now test yourself in the use of pronouns

In the following there are groups of two words in the brackets. One of the words is correct, and the other is wrong. Cross out the wrong word.

A
1 (I, Me) listened to pop-music with (she, her).
2 Her brother is taller than (we, us) are, but she is smaller than (I, me) am.
3 Between you and (I, me) no one knows the secret.
4 It is (they, them) we want to join the club.
5 I know your face. (Who, What) is your name?
6 (Who, Which) is writing his name in the book?
7 The teacher knows (we, us) are sometimes annoyed with (us, ourselves).
8 Was it (I, me) you saw at the party with (they, them)?
9 (This, That) is your book here, and (this, that) is my book over there.
10 Susan caught Becky and (she, her), but she did not catch Ann and (I, me).
11 Nicholas is cleverer than (he, him) is, but not as clever as (I, me) am.
12 This is the man (who, which) frightened (we, us).
13 I played all day with (he, him) and (she, her).
14 It curled (himself, itself) up and went to sleep.
15 Those are (they, them).

From the evidence given at the trial of the Knave of Hearts in *Alice in Wonderland* by Lewis Carroll:

1 They told me you had been to her,
2 And mentioned me to him:
3 She gave me a good character,
4 But said I could not swim.
5 He sent them word I had not gone,
6   (We know it to be true:)
7 If she should push the matter on,
8 What would become of you?

B Underline the 16 pronouns in the above verse.

C Why is the passage so difficult to understand?

. . . .

. . . .

Adjectives

An adjective is a word that adds to the meaning of a noun. It is sometimes called a 'describing' word. These words are descriptive adjectives:

fat soft beautiful cruel hard-hearted charming

Underline the descriptive adjectives in the following:

A 1 The <u>beautiful</u> princess helped the <u>frail old</u> lady to rise.
  2 The cruel wolves tracked the wounded beast across the deep snow.
  3 Into the icy water the brave man dived again and again.
  4 When the heavy lid was raised the brilliant jewels could be seen.
  5 The limping footballer scored the winning goal.

These are adjectives of quantity:
  Definite quantities: all the numerals (one, two, three and so on)
  second, third, fourth and so on
  both, double, treble and so on
  Indefinite quantities: few, some, many, all, several, any

Underline the adjectives of quantity in the following:

B 1 <u>Several</u> children took part in <u>both</u> plays.
  2 Some rain fell on the third day of the holidays.
  3 A few fish lurked under the second bridge.
  4 Many cars had double successes.
  5 All girls are expected to bring some toys to the fair.

Some adjectives put a limit on the noun.
  Demonstrative adjectives this that these those
    point out the object being talked or written about.
  Interrogative adjectives which whose what
    ask questions about some object or person.
  Distributive adjectives each every either neither a an the
    refer to individual objects or people.

Underline the limiting adjectives in the following:

C 1 This <u>cap</u> belongs to <u>neither</u> boy.
  2 That street is where every child lives.
  3 Which picture do you like best?
  4 Whose photograph hangs on the wall?
  5 The scent costs a pound an ounce.

Adjectives – degrees of comparison

The positive degree is the simple form of the adjective. It is the form shown in a dictionary entry: cold   beautiful   callous   swift   great

The comparative degree is used to compare two persons or two things:
Almost all adjectives of one syllable and many adjectives of two syllables form the comparative by adding -r or -er to the simple adjective.
cold becomes colder   swift becomes swifter   great becomes greater

Write the comparative form by the side of the simple adjective:

A 1 brave . *braver* . . . .   2 quick . . . .   3 fine . . . .

4 short . . . .   5 large . . . .   6 small . . . .

7 narrow . . . .   8 pleasant . . . .   9 shallow . . . .

Some adjectives of two syllables also add -r or -er, but spelling rules mean that changes have to be made to the simple adjectives:

ugly becomes uglier   thin becomes thinner

Many adjectives of two syllables or more form the comparative by using more before the simple adjective:

careless becomes more careless   beautiful becomes more beautiful

The superlative degree is used in comparing three or more persons or things.
Almost all adjectives of one syllable and many of two syllables form the superlative by adding -st or -est to the simple adjective:

cold becomes coldest   swift becomes swiftest   great becomes greatest

Write by the side of the simple adjective the superlative form:

B 1 brave . *bravest* . . . .   2 quick . . . .   3 fine . . . .

4 short . . . .   5 large . . . .   6 small . . . .

7 narrow . . . .   8 pleasant . . . .   9 shallow . . . .

Many adjectives of two syllables or more form the superlative by using most before the simple adjective:

Careless becomes most careless   beautiful becomes most beautiful

★ Now test yourself in the use of adjectives

Underline the adjectives in the following sentences:

A 1 The skilful driver kept his racing car steady on the slippery road.
    2 The kind lady dropped a small coin into the collecting box.
    3 The venturesome climber slipped from the narrow crumbling path.
    4 The fierce little creature attacked the terrified bird.
    5 Three boys and two girls ate several cakes each.
    6 Any girl in the fourth form would envy some lucky boys.
    7 Some people with cold hands are supposed to have warm hearts.
    8 The thief – cold-blooded, cruel and greedy – killed the little dog.
    9 Each girl took every advantage of the holiday.
  10 Those ear-rings should not be worn in this school.
  11 Whose work is this spoiled picture?
  12 Which skates belong to neither boy?

Complete the following chart.

	Positive	Comparative	Superlative
B 1	mild	. . . .	. . . .
2	beautiful	. . . .	. . . .
3	rich	. . . .	. . . .
4	simple	. . . .	. . . .
5	benevolent	. . . .	. . . .
6	fierce	. . . .	. . . .

Complete this chart which consists of adjectives compared irregularly.

	Positive	Comparative	Superlative
C 1	little	. . . .	. . . .
2	many, much	. . . .	. . . .
3	bad	. . . .	. . . .
4	good	. . . .	. . . .
5	far (for information)	. . . .	. . . .
6	far (distance)	. . . .	. . . .

Verbs

The verb is an important part of the sentence. Nearly all sentences contain a verb.

A verb may express action, such as swim, run, sing, fall, throw.
It is therefore sometimes called the 'doing' word.

Underline the verb in the following.

A 1 The boy <u>reads</u> the book.
   2 Joanne danced on to the stage.
   3 The horse neighed.
   4 The tortoise crawled slowly across the stony path.
   5 With a splash the bucket dropped into the well.
   6 Stand to attention for the officer.
   7 Before the end of the concert the choir sang two ballads.
   8 The lightning flashed and the thunder clashed.
   9 The lion quietly stalked its prey.
  10 Father wrote to the manager.

A verb may express a state of being, such as is, are, am. Other linking words that express a state or condition are feel (ill), look (smart), taste (sweet).

Underline the verb in the following:

B 1 The children <u>are</u> on the field.
   2 I am ready.
   3 The dog is in his kennel.
   4 The beaten team seems happy enough despite their defeat.
   5 The dogs are wild in the garden.
   6 The teacher sounds angry and the class grows quiet.
   7 Remain still until you are ready.
   8 The household guards look smart in their uniform.
   9 The battle seems lost.
  10 The umpire appears satisfied.

Auxiliary verbs

Sometimes we use two words to complete the verb. The lesser verbs that help the main verb are known as auxiliary verbs. Auxiliary verbs are: is, are, was, were, may, might, should, would, will, shall, can, could, do, did, had, have, has.

Underline the *two words* that complete the verb in the following:

A 1 The woman <u>has</u> <u>tried</u>.
2 The ship will arrive.
3 The boy might copy his neighbour's work.
4 I shall run all the way to the station.
5 The aeroplanes should land soon.
6 The old man was injured in the road-accident.

The auxiliary verb may be separated from the main verb by another word or words.

The cripple had never tried before.
The driver can very rarely take passengers.

Sometimes we need three words to complete a verb.

The wheel should be changed before Saturday.
The pirate has been wounded by the sailor.

Underline the verbs in the following:

B 1 The car <u>will</u> <u>be</u> <u>bought</u>.
2 You should have waited for your little sister.
3 The whistle had been blown before the goal was scored.
4 The pony jumped the wall.
5 The painting will be finished by morning.
6 The painter had nearly finished his work.
7 When the clock strikes nine the work will be done.
8 The jockey whipped his horse.
9 The lorry will go faster down the hill.
10 Come along!
11 You may want a new bike but you will never get it.
12 Stand and deliver!

Number in the Verb – singular or plural

If the subject of a sentence is singular (only one) the verb is singular.
If the subject is plural (more than one) the verb is plural.

Singular (only one): I walk, you walk, he walks, she walks, it walks
Plural (more than one): we walk, you walk, they walk

Complete the following using the correct number in the verb:

A 1 I play, he *plays*, she *plays*, it *plays*, you *play*, we *play*.

   2 I run, he runs, she . . . . . ., it . . . . . ., you . . . . . ., they . . . . . .

   3 I jump, he . . . . . ., she . . . . . ., it . . . . . ., we . . . . . ., they . . . . . .

   4 I fall, she . . . . . ., it . . . . . ., you . . . . . ., we . . . . . ., they . . . . . .

   5 I hit, he . . . . . ., she . . . . . ., you . . . . . ., they . . . . . ., we . . . . . .

   6 I . . . . . ., he writes, she . . . . . ., it . . . . . ., you . . . . . ., they. . . . . .

Note final -es (spelling rule)

   7 I catch, he catches, she . . . . . ., it . . . . . ., you . . . . . ., we . . . . . .

   8 I wish, he . . . . . ., she . . . . . ., you . . . . . ., we . . . . . ., you . . . . . .

Note change of final -y to -ies in the third person singular (spelling rule)

   9 I try, he tries, she . . . . . ., you . . . . . ., it . . . . . ., we . . . . . ., they . . . . . .

  10 I cry, he . . . . . ., she . . . . . ., you . . . . . ., we . . . . . ., they . . . . . .

Tenses in the Verb – present and past

The tense of a verb shows when an action takes place.
Present tense shows that an action takes place now or is completed now.

she walks   she is walk*ing*   she has walked   she has been walk*ing*

Note the words ending in *-ing*. They are known as present participles.
They show continuous action.
Past tense shows that an action took place yesterday or at some previous time.

she walk*ed*   she was walking   she had walk*ed*   she had been walking

The simple past tense in regular verbs is formed by adding *-ed*.
The past participle, which ends in *-ed* or can be irregular (see page 18), shows completed action.

Principal parts of irregular verbs that cause trouble

Present	Past	Past participle	Present	Past	Past participle
am, be	was	been	give	gave	given
awake	awaked	awakened	go	went	gone
	awoke		grow	grew	grown
bear	bore	borne	hear	heard	heard
begin	began	begun	hide	hid	hidden
bend	bent	bent	kneel	knelt	knelt
bite	bit	bitten	know	knew	known
blow	blew	blown	lay	laid	laid
break	broke	broken	leave	left	left
bring	brought	brought	lose	lost	lost
catch	caught	caught	make	made	made
choose	chose	chosen	pay	paid	paid
come	came	come	ride	rode	ridden
do	did	done	ring	rang	rung
draw	drew	drawn	run	ran	run
drink	drank	drunk	say	said	said
eat	ate	eaten	sell	sold	sold
fall	fell	fallen	shake	shook	shaken
feel	felt	felt	sing	sang	sung
fly	flew	flown	swim	swam	swum
forget	forgot	forgotten	tear	tore	torn
freeze	froze	frozen	write	wrote	written
get	got	got			

Using the auxiliary verbs

Except for the simple present and the simple past tenses all tenses are formed with the auxiliary verbs do, have, had, be, shall, will, should and would. In speech auxiliaries are often contracted:

   is and has become 's He's working. She's gone home.
   had and would become 'd. He'd scored. She'd often go to the pictures.

The negative is usually formed by adding not before the main verb.

   I shall not go.   She was not playing.

In a dictionary, verbs are usually shown in their infinitive form:

   (to) catch, (to) shop, (to) fly, (to) learn, (to) forget, (to) hit, (to) mark (to) climb

★ Now test yourself in the use of verbs

Underline the verbs in the following:

A 1 The detective arrested the thief.
  2 In the murky water the diver fought the octopus.
  3 Kick the ball into the goal.
  4 The farmer ploughed the field in autumn.

B 1 They had caught the lost dog.
  2 I will telephone you in the morning.
  3 The most daring of the boys would climb the tree.
  4 The team will be pleased with the result.

C 1 Once more the king is on the throne.
  2 The apple tastes sweet and the orange tastes bitter.
  3 If you feel ill tomorrow you will stay in bed.
  4 Now you are here I should really like you to stay.

Write the past tense of the following (you can use the chart on page 18):

D 1 bring . . . .   2 swim . . . .   3 kneel . . . .

  4 blow . . . .   5 say . . . .   6 lose . . . .

Write the past participle of the following:

E 1 draw . . . .   2 sell . . . .   3 lay . . . .

  4 break . . . .   5 fly . . . .   6 write . . . .

Fill each gap correctly with one of these words: know, known, knew, knows.

F 1 I . . . . the answer now.

  2 I . . . . yesterday that you were not well.

  3 I have . . . . the dog all my life.

  4 He . . . . his way to the market, and goes there every week.

  5 I will . . . . what to do when I see him tomorrow.

  6 I would like to . . . . her very much.

Adverbs

An adverb is a word that modifies or adds to the meaning of another word: a verb, an adjective or another verb.

Most adverbs are derived from adjectives by the addition of -ly.

slow becomes slowly   bad becomes badly

Write the equivalent adverb for the following adjectives:

	Adjective	Adverb		Adjective	Adverb
A 1	quick	*quickly*	2	neat	. . . .
3	loud	. . . .	4	clear	. . . .
5	free	. . . .	6	brave	. . . .

Sometimes the adverb is changed in spelling (see spelling rules).

Write the equivalent adjective for the following adverbs:

	Adjective	Adverb		Adjective	Adverb
B 1	*greedy*	greedily	2	. . . .	easily
3	. . . .	humbly	4	. . . .	gently

Some adverbs do not end in -ly. They have the same form as adjectives.

Complete each sentence with the correct adverb:

	Adjective	Sentence with adverb
C 1	a *hard* job	I worked . . *hard* . . . . to get the job finished.
2	an *early* train	The train arrived . . . . at the station.
3	a *fast* race	The girls ran . . . . to get there first.
4	a *short* stick	The wind made the ball fall . . . . of the goal.

Adverbs tell how, when, where and how much.
Adverbs of manner answer the question How?

e.g. badly, easily, slowly, well, surely, loudly, quietly, clumsily

D 1 The boys played . . *quietly* . . . . so that they should not disturb the sleeping man.
   2 Jean fell . . . . off her bike and sprained her ankle.
   3 The knight shouted . . . . to make himself heard.
   4 The tortoise crawled . . . . but still won the race.

Adverbs of time answer the question When?

e.g. today, soon, yesterday, before, now, since, seldom, often, immediately, already

Complete each sentence with one of the adverbs listed above:

A 1 He came *yesterday* . and stayed the night.

2 Start . . . . the whistle is blown.

3 We have swimming . . . . and games tomorrow.

4 Comets . . . . appear in the sky.

5 The horse has . . . . won two races before this one.

6 I will run and . . . . catch him up.

Adverbs of place answer the question Where?

e.g. here, everywhere, above, behind, outside, west, in, out, straight, nowhere

Complete each sentence with one of the adverbs listed above:

B 1 He searched *everywhere* but could not find the treasure.

2 The wind blows . . . . but the hut is snug inside.

3 The arrow went . . . . to its target.

4 The bridesmaids followed close . . . . the bride.

5 He went in dry and came . . . . wet.

6 The church spire could be seen high . . . .

Adverbs of degree answer the question How much?

e.g. almost, completely, less, thoroughly, quite, very, too, hardly, entirely, so

Complete each sentence with one of the adverbs listed above:

C 1 The tired old man walked . . *very* . . . . . slowly.

2 I have . . . . finished mowing the lawn and then I will rest.

3 When the boys are ready . . . . we will go.

4 I have . . . . money now I have finished shopping.

5 Dry your hair . . . . or you will catch cold.

6 Your work is . . . . wrong and you must do it again.

Interrogative abverbs are When? Where? Why? Relative adverbs are when, where, why.

Adverbs – degrees of comparison

Adverbs are compared in the same way as adjectives (see page 13).

The positive degree is the simple form of the adverb. It is the form shown in a dictionary entry: bravely   slowly   early   badly   much

The comparative degree is used to compare two persons or things.
The superlative degree is used to compare three or more persons or things.

Adverbs of one syllable usually form the comparative degree by adding -er and the superlative degree by adding -est

Complete this chart:

	Positive	Comparative	Superlative
A 1	soon	sooner	soonest
2	hard		
3	fast		
4	late		
5	early		

Adverbs of two syllables or more generally form the comparative by adding more and the superlative by adding most

Complete this chart:

	Positive	Comparative	Superlative
B 1	briefly	more briefly	most briefly
2	happily		
3	quickly		
4	carefully		
5	easily		

Complete this chart of exceptions:

		Comparative	Superlative
C 1	badly, ill	worse	worst
2	far		
3	little		
4	much, many		
5	well		

★ Now test yourself in the use of adverbs

Underline the adverbs in the following:

A 1 The footballers will soon be ready and the match can begin.
2 The girl formerly lived with her grandmother.
3 The fox withdrew quickly into the wood.
4 The children behaved badly at the circus.
5 Jennifer once heard a mouse in the cupboard.
6 Where was the escaped prisoner hiding?

Complete the following with adverbs from this list: gleefully impudently, smartly, bitterly, greedily, lovingly, fitfully, tunefully

B 1 The cheeky boy answered . . . .   2 The sentry saluted . . . .

3 He chuckled . . . .   4 The hungry boy ate . . . .

5 The cat was caressed . . . .   6 The choir sang . . . .

7 The dog slept . . . .   8 The wind blew . . . .

Complete the following chart:

	Positive	Comparative	Superlative
C 1	willingly	. . . .	. . . .
2	ill	. . . .	. . . .
3	early	. . . .	. . . .
4	loudly	. . . .	. . . .
5	seriously	. . . .	. . . .
6	fearfully	. . . .	. . . .

Complete the following with the correct comparatives and superlatives of these adverbs: closely, quickly, late, brightly, hard, carefully.

D 1 You walked quickly but John walked . . . .

2 We both moved carefully, but I moved . . . . than you.

3 The lights shone brightly, but the stage lights shone . . . .

4 He looked at the insect closely, and then he looked . . . . still.

5 I tried hard, but Jill tried even . . . .

6 I came late, but Susan was the . . . . to arrive.

Conjunctions

Conjunctions join together words or word groups.

Here are six simple conjunctions that are used to join together groups of words of equal value: and but for nor or yet

Complete each of the following with the most suitable conjunction from the list above:

A 1 Katie . *and* .... Maggie are friends.

2 He was a giant, ... he was weak.

3 He expected presents, ... it was his birthday.

4 The book was not on the shelves, ... was it on the desk.

5 I will smile if we win .... if we lose.

6 We quarrel ... *but* ... we are friends.

Some conjunctions are used in pairs: both ... and, so ... as, either ... or, neither ... nor whether ... or

Complete each of the following with the most suitable conjunction from the pairs listed above:

B 1 <u>Both</u> the highwayman . *and* ... the innkeeper were guilty.

2 The goal was missed by .... the striker and the winger.

3 Would you be so good .... to repeat the directions?

4 Either you will confess .. *or* ..... I will tell the whole story.

5 .... Freddie nor Lynn wants to go to the party.

6 It does not matter to me whether you play ... *or* ..... not.

Underline both conjunctions in each sentence above.

Conjunctions can be grouped according to their special meanings.
They can express *Time, Place, Reason, Concession, Condition, Manner, Purpose, Result*.

Time when while as since till until after before whenever
Place where wherever
Reason because since as
Concession although though while as even if whether ... or

Condition if unless
Manner as, as if as . . . as so . . . as than as though
Purpose so that
Result so . . . that

Complete the following sentences to make sense.
Underline the conjunctions.

A 1 <u>When</u> the pie was opened, the birds . *began to sing.* . . . .

   2 You must wash your hands before . . . .

   3 After you have eaten your supper . . . .

   4 I have not spoken to her since . . . .

   5 . . . . until you come.

   6 . . . . while the cat was asleep.

   7 As the dog barked . . . .

   8 I shall not see him till . . . .

B 1 He found the ball where . . . .

   2 Wherever the old man went . . . .

   3 I shall not come to the party because . . . .

   4 . . . . since you cannot hear.

   5 As it is Bonfire Night . . . .

C 1 I will not go to town even if . . . .

   2 Although she asked the pianist to play . . . .

   3 You will take part whether . . . . or not.

   4 Judy will not swim in the pool unless . . . .

   5 If the shop is open . . . .

   6 I opened the gate into the field so that . . . .

   7 She acted the lady as if . . . .

   8 As quick as lightning . . . .

Prepositions

Most prepositions are short words (to, on, for). Some prepositions are longer words (underneath, alongside). Some prepositions are even groups of words (as far as, in spite of).
Prepositions are normally placed before nouns or pronouns. They show the relation of one word (usually a noun or a pronoun) to some other word in the sentence.

The cat is on the mat. (on shows the position of the cat)
The cat walked towards its basket. (towards shows direction)
The cat goes out after dark. (after shows the time when the cat goes out)

The most common prepositions are:

up   down   in   on   at   with   of   for   over   by   between   towards   to

Complete the following adding the most suitable preposition from the list above.

A 1 We arrived ...*on*...... Monday.

2 The girl curtseyed and gave the bouquet .... the queen.

3 The ship sailed .... the desert island.

4 The firemen slid .... the poles.

5 The salmon leapt .... the waterfall.

6 Mother placed the meat .... the two slices of bread.

7 The mountaineer climbed .... the vertical cliff.

8 The swimmer swam every day .... the pool.

9 The young girl looked .... her reflection in the water.

Write three suitable and different prepositions for each sentence.

B 1 The book lay ...*in*...... the box.

2 The book lay .... the box.

3 The book lay .... the box.

4 The skier raced .... the flags.

5 The skier raced .... the flags.

6 The skier raced .... the flags.

More prepositions

The following list consists of common prepositions:

  about   after   from   to   within

Complete the following adding the most suitable preposition from each list:

A 1 The tortoise tucked its head . *within* . . . . the shell.

  2 The boxer struck his opponent . . . . the bell sounded.

  3 The park is open . . . . dawn . . . . dusk.

  4 The mice ran . . . . the granary floor.

  round   until   into   under   past

B 1 Gather . . *round* . . . and listen to my story.

  2 Go . . . . the wood . . . . you come to the blasted oak.

  3 It is now . . . . bedtime.

  4 You will find the house key . . . . the mat.

  above   near   till   below   off

C 1 The stain can be seen . *above* . . . . the window but . . *below* . . . . . the roof.

  2 We will not go home . . . . morning.

  3 The tiger is now . . . . the hunters.

  4 I switched . . . . the light and sat in the dark.

These are prepositions formed from groups of words:

  because of   due to   except for   away from
  on top of   in front of   by means of   out of

Complete the following from the list above:

D 1 I shall not come *because of* . . my mother's illness.

  2 All the children played . . . . Sam and Charles.

  3 This is the money . . . . you for meals.

  4 Do not stand . . . . the camera.

  5 Get . . . . the kicking horse or you will be hurt.

  6 The flag flew . . . . the church spire.

  7 I saw her when she came . . . . the shadows.

  8 They entered the castle . . . . the secret passage.

27

Interjections

The interjection is a word of exclamation that expresses emotion or feeling. It is sometimes shown by itself followed by an exclamation mark.

Oh! (surprise) Ugh! (pain) Nonsense! (disgust) Hurrah! (pleasant excitement) Ah! (satisfaction) Ouch! (pain) Ooh! (pain and pleasure) Aha! (great satisfaction) Oh dear! (consternation) What! (anger) Help! (despair) H'm! (thought) Indeed! (surprise)

Complete the following adding the most suitable interjection from the list above:

A 1 ..Nonsense!...... That was a silly remark to make.

   2 .... We have reached our destination at last.

   3 .... I'm very, very hot!

   4 .... You did surprise me.

   5 .... I am drowning!

   6 .... You again – you drive me mad!

The interjection is sometimes included in a sentence. It begins the sentence, and the exclamation mark comes at the end of the sentence. The interjection is followed by a comma, and the sentence explains the emotion – the reason for the exclamation.

Complete the following adding the most suitable interjection from the list at the top of the page:

B 1 ......Ah!........., I can see you!

   2 ...., you kicked me!

   3 ...., I thought you said that!

   4 ...., what beautiful chocolates!

   5 ...., what shall I do with you!

   6 ...., now I have caught you!

Articles

the is the definite article and is used for a particular thing.
a (before consonants) and an (before a vowel) are indefinite articles.
Complete this sentence:

C The clown climbed ...... pole eating ...... apple and ...... banana.

★ Now test yourself in conjunctions, prepositions and interjections

Complete the following with the most suitable conjunction:

A   1   The horse galloped across the field .... jumped the gate.

    2   The chairman spoke .... he closed the meeting.

    3   You will wait here .... the order is given to go.

    4   Post the notice .... everyone will be able to see it.

    5   We must run .... we are late.

    6   .... I have told him many times he still climbs the tree.

    7   You must go .... you are invited or not.

    8   Let me know .... you want to play.

    9   The opossum can act .... it were dead.

   10   The speaker shouted .... everyone in the vast crowd could hear.

Complete the following with the most suitable preposition:

B   1   The sailor swam .... the drowning man.

    2   The boys climbed .... the greasy pole.

    3   The tired old man leaned .... the wall.

    4   The osprey dived .... the river and caught a fish.

    5   The cashier placed the bags of money .... the counter.

    6   The clown walked .... the tightrope.

    7   The treasure was hidden .... the rubble.

    8   The motor cyclist rode .... the wall of fire.

    9   The paper was wrapped .... the parcel.

   10   The dog jumped .... the fence and escaped.

Complete the following with the most suitable interjection:

C   1   ...., what a shock you gave me.

    2   ....! It is hot near the fire.

    3   ...., I saw you that time.

    4   .... dear! I have forgotten to bring my money.

    5   ...., that's the kind of apple I like.

★ Now test yourself and check your rating

Read this story:

A *little girl* was painting *industriously* a *picture* of her *favourite meal*. She *carefully painted* a *delicious plate* of *rich crisp chips, baked beans*, white and yellow *fried eggs* and *sizzling fat sausages*. The *teacher* said that she *could show* the picture to the *class* when she *had finished* it.

The girl painted until the picture *was finished*. Then she *proudly showed* the picture to the class. The class *gasped*, "Oh!" All the painting *was covered* with *red paint*.

"What a *terrible* thing *to do*!" said the teacher *angrily*. "Who *did* it?"

"I did," *said* the little girl. "It's *tomato sauce*. I always *have* lots of tomato sauce. I *love* it."

Write twelve nouns from the words in *italics* in the story above:

A 1 . . . .   2 . . . .   3 . . . .   4 . . . .

   5 . . . .   6 . . . .   7 . . . .   8 . . . .

   9 . . . .   10 . . . .   11 . . . .   12 . . . .

Write twelve verbs (some have more than one word) from the words in *italics* in the story:

B 1 . . . .   2 . . . .   3 . . . .   4 . . . .

   5 . . . .   6 . . . .   7 . . . .   8 . . . .

   9 . . . .   10 . . . .   11 . . . .   12 . . . .

Write twelve adjectives from the words in *italics* in the story above:

C 1 . . . .   2 . . . .   3 . . . .   4 . . . .

   5 . . . .   6 . . . .   7 . . . .   8 . . . .

   9 . . . .   10 . . . .   11 . . . .   12 . . . .

Write four adverbs from the words in *italics* in the story above:

D 1 . . . .   2 . . . .   3 . . . .   4 . . . .

Answers

Now test yourself (nouns) (page 8)

A 1 child; 2 goose; 3 box; 4 man; 5 passer-by; 6 tooth.

B 1 women; 2 sheep; 3 loaves; 4 echoes; 5 mouse-traps; 6 feet.

C 1 god; 2 husband; 3 bridegroom; 4 emperor; 5 nephew; 6 male.

D 1 lioness; 2 aunt; 3 witch; 4 traitress; 5 nun; 6 headmistress.

E 1 leopardess, cub; 2 boar, piglet; 3 ewe, lamb; 4 bull, cow.

F 1 army; 2 herd; 3 flock; 4 pack; 5 clutch; 6 flight; 7 truss; 8 suite.

G 1 audience; 2 congregation; 3 passengers; 4 customers.

H 1 hand; 2 peal or ring; 3 punnet; 4 group.

Now test yourself (pronouns) (page 11)

A 1 I, her; 2 we, I; 3 me; 4 they; 5 what; 6 who: 7 we, ourselves;
8 me, them; 9 this, that; 10 her, me; 11 he, I; 12 who, us; 13 him,
her; 14 itself; 15 they.

B 1 they, me, you, her; 2 me, him; 3 she, me; 4 I; 5 he, them, I; 6 we, it; 7 she;
8 you.

C We do not know to what or to whom the pronouns apply.

Now test yourself (adjectives) (page 14)

A 1 skilful, racing, slippery; 2 kind, small, collecting; 3 venturesome, narrow, crumbling;
4 fierce, little, terrified; 5 three, two, several; 6 any, fourth, lucky; 7 some, cold,
warm; 8 cold-blooded, cruel, greedy, little; 9 each, every; 10 those, this; 11 whose,
spoiled; 12 which, neither.

B 1 milder, mildest; 2 more, most; 3 richer, richest; 4 simpler, simplest; 5 more, most;
6 fiercer, fiercest.

C 1 less, least; 2 more, most; 3 worse, worst; 4 better, best; 5 further, furthest;
6 farther, farthest.

Now test yourself (verbs) (page 19)

A 1 arrested; 2 fought; 3 kick; 4 ploughed.

B 1 had caught; 2 will telephone; 3 would climb; 4 will be pleased.

C 1 is; 2 tastes, tastes; 3 feel ill, will stay; 4 are, should like, to stay.

D 1 brought; 2 swam; 3 knelt; 4 blew; 5 said; 6 lost.

E 1 drawn; 2 sold; 3 laid; 4 broken; 5 flown; 6 written.

F 1 know; 2 knew; 3 known; 4 knows; 5 know; 6 know.

Now test yourself (adverbs) (page 23)

A 1 soon; 2 formerly; 3 quickly; 4 badly; 5 once; 6 where.

B 1 impudently; 2 smartly; 3 gleefully; 4 greedily; 5 lovingly; 6 tunefully; 7 fitfully;
8 bitterly.

C 1 more, most; 2 iller, illest; or worse, worst; 3 earlier, earliest; 4 more, most; 5 more,
most; 6 more, most.

D 1 more quickly; 2 more carefully; 3 brightest; 4 more closely; 5 harder; 6 latest.

Now test yourself (conjunctions, prepositions and interjections) (page 29)

A 1 and; 2 before; 3 until; 4 where; 5 because; 6 although (though); 7 whether;
8 if; 9 as if; 10 so that.

B 1 to; 2 up; 3 against; 4 into; 5 on; 6 along; 7 beneath (under, underneath);
   8 through; 9 round; 10 over.
C 1 Oh; 2 Phew; 3 Aha; 4 Oh; 5 Ah.

Now test yourself (page 30) (Check your rating.)
Count five points for each correct answer. You could score 200 points for all-correct answers.

Nouns A 1 girl; 2 picture; 3 meal; 4 plate; 5 chips; 6 beans; 7 eggs; 8 sausages;
   9 teacher; 10 class; 11 paint; 12 sauce.

Verbs B 1 painted; 2 could show; 3 had finished; 4 was finished; 5 showed;
   6 gasped; 7 was covered; 8 to do; 9 did; 10 said; 11 have; 12 love.

Adjectives C 1 little; 2 favourite; 3 delicious; 4 rich; 5 crisp; 6 baked; 7 fried;
   8 sizzling; 9 fat; 10 red; 11 terrible; 12 tomato.

Adverbs D 1 industriously; 2 carefully; 3 proudly; 4 angrily.

Rating Chart
175 to 200: Excellent.
150 to 175: Very good indeed.
125 to 150: Good.
100 to 125: Fair.
Below 100: Check your mistakes. Try the exercises again.

ISBN 0 340 50574 5

This Headway edition first published 1989

Fourth impression 1991

Copyright © Boswell Taylor

Printed in Great Britain for the educational publishing division of
Hodder & Stoughton Ltd, Mill Road, Dunton Green, Sevenoaks, Kent by
CW Print Group, Loughton, Essex.